Rockhounding Mineral Log

Published in Colorado Springs, Colorado by Donley S. Collins

ISBN 978-1-7374699-9-5

Cover Design and interior formatting by:

Elizabeth Harper at EHR Ltd.

elizabethharperreads@gmail.com

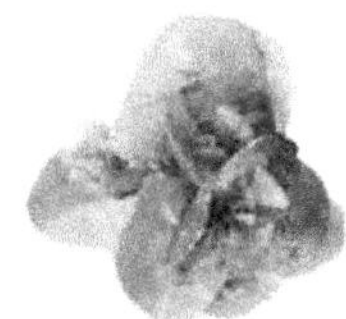

Table of Contents for Mineral Log Locations

Table of Contents for Mineral Log Locations

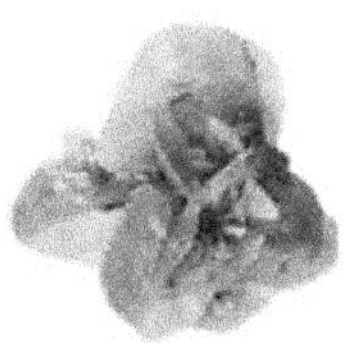

Trip Location	Mineral	Page

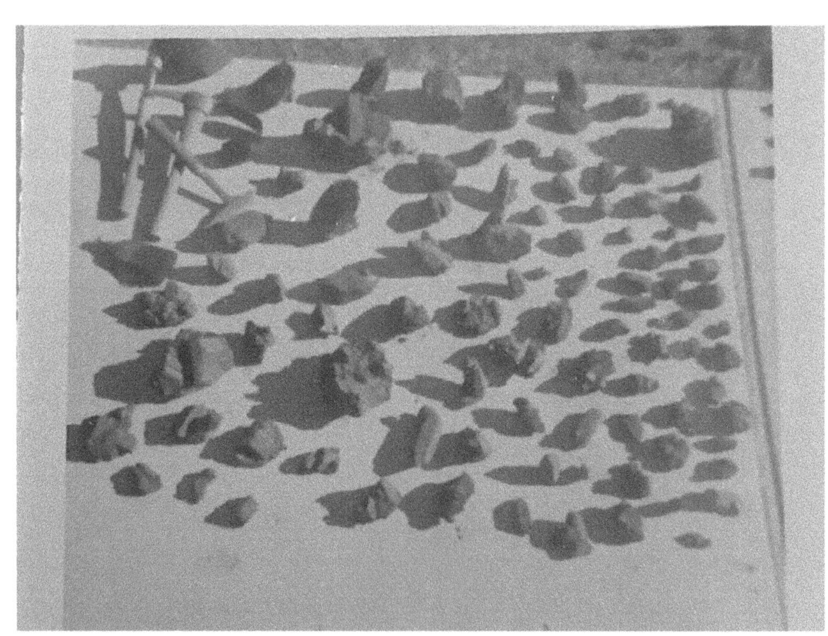

Log of Mineral Locations

LOCATION AND DIRECTION

Lake George Quad. Colorado. Near the Old Stage? Stop. R7/W T12 us. Sec 221/4 SE

Start Colorado Springs. Go West on HWY 24 to Lake George. Then pass Ranger Station Rd NE. Then take left to Old Stage Stop. STOP. Hill to east of station is small, elongated hill (trending about N-S).

DATE DISCOVERED

Summer of 1969

MAP OF LOCATION

GPS

LONGITUDE

-105.315663

LATITUDE

38.988623

NOTES

MINERALS FOUND IN THE AREA

Smoky Quartz, microcline, limonite?

pseudo-after magnetite, leucite and amazonite.

Bob recovered 5lb smoky quartz XL from this pocket

Later in the summer a large Topaz-Blue on hill due south of the

Stage Station was found.

GEOLOGICAL DATA

Peg in ring dike

* This site is now closed to the public.

Remember to always check. You may need to get prior permission before you go exploring and dig.

LOCATION AND DIRECTION

DATE DISCOVERED

MAP OF LOCATION	GPS

LONGITUDE

LATITUDE

NOTES

MINERALS FOUND IN THE AREA

GEOLOGICAL DATA

Log of Mineral Locations

LOCATION AND DIRECTION

DATE DISCOVERED

MAP OF LOCATION	GPS

LONGITUDE

LATITUDE

NOTES

MINERALS FOUND IN THE AREA

GEOLOGICAL DATA

Log of Mineral Locations

LOCATION AND DIRECTION

DATE DISCOVERED

MAP OF LOCATION | GPS

N

LONGITUDE

LATITUDE

NOTES

MINERALS FOUND IN THE AREA

GEOLOGICAL DATA

Log of Mineral Locations

LOCATION AND DIRECTION

DATE DISCOVERED

MAP OF LOCATION	GPS

N

LONGITUDE

LATITUDE

NOTES

MINERALS FOUND IN THE AREA

GEOLOGICAL DATA

Log of Mineral Locations

LOCATION AND DIRECTION

DATE DISCOVERED

MAP OF LOCATION | GPS

N

LONGITUDE

LATITUDE

NOTES

MINERALS FOUND IN THE AREA

GEOLOGICAL DATA

LOCATION AND DIRECTION

DATE DISCOVERED

MAP OF LOCATION

GPS

LONGITUDE

LATITUDE

NOTES

MINERALS FOUND IN THE AREA

GEOLOGICAL DATA

LOCATION AND DIRECTION

DATE DISCOVERED

MAP OF LOCATION | GPS

LONGITUDE

LATITUDE

NOTES

MINERALS FOUND IN THE AREA

GEOLOGICAL DATA

Log of Mineral Locations

LOCATION AND DIRECTION

DATE DISCOVERED

MAP OF LOCATION	GPS

LONGITUDE

LATITUDE

NOTES

MINERALS FOUND IN THE AREA

GEOLOGICAL DATA

LOCATION AND DIRECTION

DATE DISCOVERED

MAP OF LOCATION | GPS

LONGITUDE

LATITUDE

NOTES

MINERALS FOUND IN THE AREA

GEOLOGICAL DATA

Log of Mineral Locations

LOCATION AND DIRECTION

DATE DISCOVERED

MAP OF LOCATION	GPS

N

LONGITUDE

LATITUDE

NOTES

MINERALS FOUND IN THE AREA

GEOLOGICAL DATA

Log of Mineral Locations

LOCATION AND DIRECTION

DATE DISCOVERED

MAP OF LOCATION

GPS

N

LONGITUDE

LATITUDE

NOTES

MINERALS FOUND IN THE AREA

GEOLOGICAL DATA

LOCATION AND DIRECTION

DATE DISCOVERED

MAP OF LOCATION	GPS

LONGITUDE

LATITUDE

NOTES

MINERALS FOUND IN THE AREA

GEOLOGICAL DATA

Log of Mineral Locations

LOCATION AND DIRECTION

DATE DISCOVERED

MAP OF LOCATION | GPS

LONGITUDE

LATITUDE

NOTES

MINERALS FOUND IN THE AREA

GEOLOGICAL DATA

LOCATION AND DIRECTION

DATE DISCOVERED

| MAP OF LOCATION | GPS |

LONGITUDE

LATITUDE

NOTES

MINERALS FOUND IN THE AREA

GEOLOGICAL DATA

LOCATION AND DIRECTION

DATE DISCOVERED

MAP OF LOCATION	GPS

N

LONGITUDE

LATITUDE

NOTES

MINERALS FOUND IN THE AREA

GEOLOGICAL DATA

LOCATION AND DIRECTION

DATE DISCOVERED

MAP OF LOCATION | GPS

N

LONGITUDE

LATITUDE

NOTES

MINERALS FOUND IN THE AREA

GEOLOGICAL DATA

PHOTOS

Log of Mineral Locations

LOCATION AND DIRECTION

DATE DISCOVERED

MAP OF LOCATION	GPS

LONGITUDE

LATITUDE

NOTES

MINERALS FOUND IN THE AREA

GEOLOGICAL DATA

LOCATION AND DIRECTION

DATE DISCOVERED

MAP OF LOCATION

GPS

LONGITUDE

LATITUDE

NOTES

MINERALS FOUND IN THE AREA

GEOLOGICAL DATA

Log of Mineral Locations

LOCATION AND DIRECTION

DATE DISCOVERED

MAP OF LOCATION | GPS

N

LONGITUDE

LATITUDE

NOTES

MINERALS FOUND IN THE AREA

GEOLOGICAL DATA

LOCATION AND DIRECTION

DATE DISCOVERED

| MAP OF LOCATION | GPS |

N

LONGITUDE

LATITUDE

NOTES

MINERALS FOUND IN THE AREA

GEOLOGICAL DATA

LOCATION AND DIRECTION

DATE DISCOVERED

MAP OF LOCATION	GPS

LONGITUDE

LATITUDE

NOTES

MINERALS FOUND IN THE AREA

GEOLOGICAL DATA

Log of Mineral Locations

LOCATION AND DIRECTION

DATE DISCOVERED

MAP OF LOCATION

| GPS |

LONGITUDE

LATITUDE

NOTES

MINERALS FOUND IN THE AREA

GEOLOGICAL DATA

PHOTOS

Log of Mineral Locations

LOCATION AND DIRECTION

DATE DISCOVERED

MAP OF LOCATION	GPS

N

LONGITUDE

LATITUDE

NOTES

MINERALS FOUND IN THE AREA

GEOLOGICAL DATA

LOCATION AND DIRECTION

DATE DISCOVERED

MAP OF LOCATION	GPS

LONGITUDE

LATITUDE

NOTES

MINERALS FOUND IN THE AREA

GEOLOGICAL DATA

LOCATION AND DIRECTION

DATE DISCOVERED

MAP OF LOCATION | GPS

N

LONGITUDE

LATITUDE

NOTES

MINERALS FOUND IN THE AREA

GEOLOGICAL DATA

LOCATION AND DIRECTION

DATE DISCOVERED

MAP OF LOCATION | GPS

LONGITUDE

LATITUDE

NOTES

MINERALS FOUND IN THE AREA

GEOLOGICAL DATA

Log of Mineral Locations

LOCATION AND DIRECTION

DATE DISCOVERED

MAP OF LOCATION

GPS

LONGITUDE

LATITUDE

NOTES

MINERALS FOUND IN THE AREA

GEOLOGICAL DATA

LOCATION AND DIRECTION

DATE DISCOVERED

MAP OF LOCATION	GPS

LONGITUDE

LATITUDE

NOTES

MINERALS FOUND IN THE AREA

GEOLOGICAL DATA

LOCATION AND DIRECTION

DATE DISCOVERED

MAP OF LOCATION | GPS

N

LONGITUDE

LATITUDE

NOTES

MINERALS FOUND IN THE AREA

GEOLOGICAL DATA

LOCATION AND DIRECTION

DATE DISCOVERED

MAP OF LOCATION | GPS

LONGITUDE

LATITUDE

NOTES

MINERALS FOUND IN THE AREA

GEOLOGICAL DATA

Log of Mineral Locations

LOCATION AND DIRECTION

DATE DISCOVERED

MAP OF LOCATION

GPS

LONGITUDE

LATITUDE

NOTES

MINERALS FOUND IN THE AREA

GEOLOGICAL DATA

LOCATION AND DIRECTION

DATE DISCOVERED

MAP OF LOCATION	GPS

LONGITUDE

LATITUDE

NOTES

MINERALS FOUND IN THE AREA

GEOLOGICAL DATA

LOCATION AND DIRECTION

DATE DISCOVERED

MAP OF LOCATION

GPS

LONGITUDE

LATITUDE

NOTES

MINERALS FOUND IN THE AREA

GEOLOGICAL DATA

Log of Mineral Locations

LOCATION AND DIRECTION

DATE DISCOVERED

MAP OF LOCATION

| GPS |

LONGITUDE

LATITUDE

NOTES

MINERALS FOUND IN THE AREA

GEOLOGICAL DATA

Log of Mineral Locations

LOCATION AND DIRECTION

DATE DISCOVERED

MAP OF LOCATION | GPS

N

LONGITUDE

LATITUDE

NOTES

MINERALS FOUND IN THE AREA

GEOLOGICAL DATA

LOCATION AND DIRECTION

DATE DISCOVERED

MAP OF LOCATION

GPS

N

LONGITUDE

LATITUDE

NOTES

MINERALS FOUND IN THE AREA

GEOLOGICAL DATA

Log of Mineral Locations

LOCATION AND DIRECTION

DATE DISCOVERED

MAP OF LOCATION

GPS

LONGITUDE

LATITUDE

NOTES

MINERALS FOUND IN THE AREA

GEOLOGICAL DATA

LOCATION AND DIRECTION

DATE DISCOVERED

MAP OF LOCATION | GPS

N

LONGITUDE

LATITUDE

NOTES

MINERALS FOUND IN THE AREA

GEOLOGICAL DATA

LOCATION AND DIRECTION

DATE DISCOVERED

MAP OF LOCATION

GPS

LONGITUDE

LATITUDE

NOTES

MINERALS FOUND IN THE AREA

GEOLOGICAL DATA

LOCATION AND DIRECTION

DATE DISCOVERED

MAP OF LOCATION

GPS

N

LONGITUDE

LATITUDE

NOTES

MINERALS FOUND IN THE AREA

GEOLOGICAL DATA

LOCATION AND DIRECTION

DATE DISCOVERED

MAP OF LOCATION | GPS

N

LONGITUDE

LATITUDE

NOTES

MINERALS FOUND IN THE AREA

GEOLOGICAL DATA

LOCATION AND DIRECTION

DATE DISCOVERED

MAP OF LOCATION | GPS

LONGITUDE

LATITUDE

NOTES

MINERALS FOUND IN THE AREA

GEOLOGICAL DATA

LOCATION AND DIRECTION

DATE DISCOVERED

MAP OF LOCATION	GPS

N

LONGITUDE

LATITUDE

NOTES

MINERALS FOUND IN THE AREA

GEOLOGICAL DATA

PHOTOS

LOCATION AND DIRECTION

DATE DISCOVERED

MAP OF LOCATION	GPS

N

LONGITUDE

LATITUDE

NOTES

MINERALS FOUND IN THE AREA

GEOLOGICAL DATA

LOCATION AND DIRECTION

DATE DISCOVERED

MAP OF LOCATION | GPS

N

LONGITUDE

LATITUDE

NOTES

MINERALS FOUND IN THE AREA

GEOLOGICAL DATA

LOCATION AND DIRECTION

DATE DISCOVERED

MAP OF LOCATION	GPS

N

LONGITUDE

LATITUDE

NOTES

MINERALS FOUND IN THE AREA

GEOLOGICAL DATA

Log of Mineral Locations

LOCATION AND DIRECTION

DATE DISCOVERED

MAP OF LOCATION | GPS

N

LONGITUDE

LATITUDE

NOTES

MINERALS FOUND IN THE AREA

GEOLOGICAL DATA

LOCATION AND DIRECTION

DATE DISCOVERED

MAP OF LOCATION | GPS

N

LONGITUDE

LATITUDE

NOTES

MINERALS FOUND IN THE AREA

GEOLOGICAL DATA

Log of Mineral Locations

LOCATION AND DIRECTION

DATE DISCOVERED

MAP OF LOCATION

GPS

LONGITUDE

LATITUDE

N

NOTES

MINERALS FOUND IN THE AREA

GEOLOGICAL DATA

LOCATION AND DIRECTION

DATE DISCOVERED

MAP OF LOCATION | GPS

LONGITUDE

LATITUDE

NOTES

MINERALS FOUND IN THE AREA

GEOLOGICAL DATA

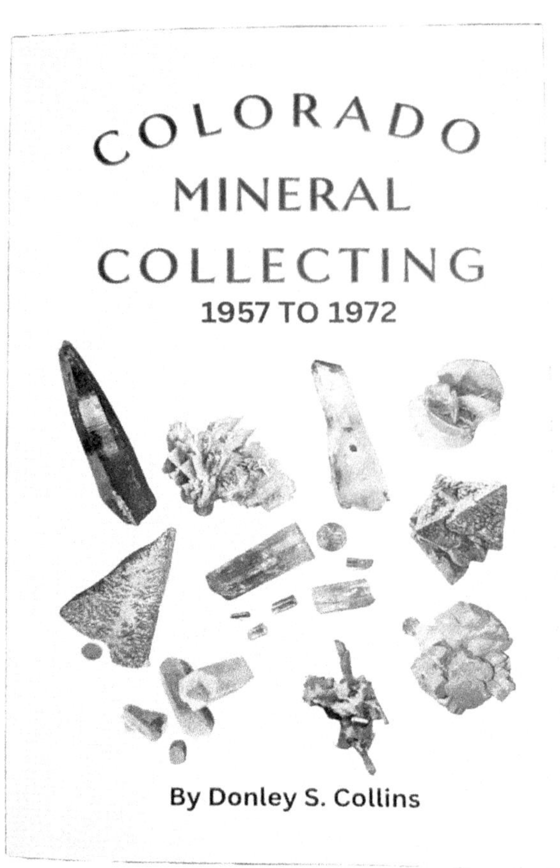

Donley S. Collins is a historical figure in the Colorado rock-hounding scene. He has spent decades with the Colorado Springs Mineralogical Society and 24 years with the United States Geological Survey specializing in stratigraphy, geomorphology, and sedimentary and igneous petrology. His expertise is reflected in over 45+ publications and abstracts.

Don's most recent project is his book
Colorado Mineral Collection 1957-1972.
Stories of great finds and encouragement for future exploration.

*AUTHOR NOTE:
Colorado is popular for gems like Aquamarine, Rhodochrosite, Fluorite, Topaz, and Quartz. They can be found on National Forests/BLM lands, but personal use only, and/or permits are often needed.
Please get needed permissions before digging.

COLORADO MINERAL COLLECTING 1957-1972 CAN BE ORDERED THROUGH MOST MAJOR BOOK SELLERS OR INGRAMSPARKS CATALOG

www.ingramcontent.com/pod-product-compliance
Lightning Source LLC
Chambersburg PA
CBHW041034050726
47599CB00018B/1960